My Sister Helped Me Heal

Vol. 3

Visionary: Chavon Anette

Copyright © 2022 by Chavon Thomas

ISBN: 979-8-218-05348-2

Cover Design: iambiancabrown.com

Printed in the USA:

All rights reserved. No part of this book may be reproduced or used in any manner without written permission of the copyright owner except for the use of quotations in a book review.

For more information, address: www.chavonanette.com

Dedication

To God Who has made this journey possible: healing, breakthrough, and deliverance.

Table of Contents

FOREWORD	i
CHAPTER 1 - SURVIVING THE SILENCE OF HEAVEN *Crystal Arrington*	1
CHAPTER 2 - MY SISTER HELPED ME HEAL *Nakia Triplett*	5
CHAPTER 3 - SISTERHOOD: A TRUE DEFINITION OF A DIVINE CONNECTION *Cecelyn Dennis*	11
CHAPTER 4 - IT'S NOTHING LIKE SISTERHOOD *Monique Weeks*	17
CHAPTER 5 - YOU WAITED LONG ENOUGH *Letitia Council*	21
CHAPTER 6 - SEEING BEYOND WHAT YOU'RE SAYING IT'S IN THE EYES OR THE EYES HAVE IT *Tracy Manley*	25
CHAPTER 7 - MY SISTER FOUGHT FOR ME *Apostle Michelle Franklin*	31
CHAPTER 8 - COMING OUT OF THE SHADOWS *Karen Downing*	35
CHAPTER 9 - I GAVE HIM MY YES! LEAVING REJECTION BEHIND! *Leah Austin*	39
CHAPTER 10 - BIRTHING THE PAIN THROUGH VICTORY *Marsha Johnson-Rollins*	43
CHAPTER 11 - MY TRANSPARENCY, THEIR LOVE: THE TALE OF MANY CAPS *Melissa Daughtry*	49
CHAPTER 12 - MY GRANDMOTHER HELPED ME HEAL *Prophetess Deleigh Ryan*	53
EPILOGUE - IT WAS NECESSARY	57

Foreword

"Relax. Take a deep breath in… and exhale it out. Let your shoulders drop, unclench your jaw and breathe. Healing has come!"

These are the words that I heard as I sat down to write this foreword. I'm not sure if you know why you were drawn to this book, but I believe God led you to it because there's a measure of healing He desires to bring to your life. Healing from old traumas and hurts, weaponized words and control, oppression and isolation. Yes, the Father has come to heal those hidden areas in you.

How can this be? you ask. *I'm just reading a book!* Allow me to remind you of the words of Revelation 12:11, which in the AMP version states, "And they overcame and conquered him because of the blood of the Lamb and because of the word of their testimony, for they did not love their life and renounce their faith even when faced with death."

While yes, your personal story or testimony may not be captured in the pages of this book, you will find bits and pieces of your life's testimony on each page. While your story is not their story, your healing will come as you read. As you take in the words of triumph that lace each page, you too will find the strength to conquer and overcome what you've quietly battled for years.

So, I encourage you to come back and read these few pages every time you pick up this book because I declare that there will be a healing balm applied to your life from each section of this book. Expect it! Take it in!

Whew! It is an honor to be a part of such a great work. The "My Sister Helped Me Heal" series is a life-changing work for both the authors, the readers, and the visionary. I've had the privilege of standing on the sideline of Chavon Anette's journey over the last few years, so allow me to share my truths and brag on her a bit.

Chavon Anette is a force unrivaled. Her fiery, spirit-filled teaching and preaching are enough to melt the strongest of mountains. Ironically, her gentleness and care possess the same ability to break down the strongest walls. With her entire being, she LOVES God and the people she's called to serve. She has the sweetest spirit and is genuinely kind to everyone she comes in contact with. Therefore, it was no surprise that what began as a casual "good morning" and "have a good week" acquaintanceship in the church between her and me quickly developed into a sisterly bond that I treasure today.

Chavon fully yielded to her divine lane of expertise a few years ago, and everything and everyone around her shifted for the better because of it. I remember the day I saw it for myself. She invited me in to be a guest on her talk show, and it was *FIRE* from the opening of the show to the closing. What was undeniable during the conversation was she had done the work, spent time with the Father, and **Intentionally Healed**! Don't get me wrong, God can use anyone and anything to accomplish His will, but there's no limit to what God can do with a HEALED WOMAN!! Chavon Anette is a Healed Woman!

This is what grants her the authority to spearhead the "My Sister Helped Me Heal" series. She went first. She humbled herself before the Father, surrendered to his healing methods, and found freedom in sisterhood. I am grateful that because of her "YES," I and many others have also experienced the healing power of sisterhood.

It's your turn! Breathe, Read, and Heal. Enjoy your journey.

Ciara Mason
Founder, Razing Women

Chapter 1

Surviving the Silence of Heaven
Crystal Arrington

"Trials teach us what we are; they dig up the soil and let us see what we are made of." - Charles Spurgeon

I'm not sure if I've told this story out loud other than repeating it multiple times in a dark room with detectives and police officers, but my prayer is that it gives you language for the season you are in. Time was winding down, and I had yet another 15-page paper to type and another final to finish. The pressure to complete all my assignments was weighing on me as I attempted to type one more page. The library was filled with frustrated college students and exhausted staff members ready to call it a night after a week of crammed assignments and deadlines. I checked my watch as my alarm went off to signal that it was midnight and that I needed to head back home to ensure I was well rested for my 8 am chemistry final. I sent a quick text to my dad to let him know I was headed home and would let him know when I made it in safely. I began to gather my belongings and head to the parking garage as I was met with a middle-aged man who was walking his dog. We had a brief conversation before I continued to head toward my car, and before I knew it, my face was pinned to the ground.

Chapter 1

My body went limp as I felt a cool breeze on my legs and back. Time stood still. I couldn't move, I couldn't scream, I couldn't hear anything—just silence. I prayed at that moment that someone would see me and rescue me. The weight of his body broke my wrists and my spirit into pieces that night. I don't remember much about what happened from when I was on the floor until I walked to the campus police station, but I do remember the silence. It was loud, and it was lonely. I wanted to get answers from God immediately but heard nothing.

Time was still a blur as I was taken into a room for questioning and met with an officer who will always be remembered as the "gentle giant" In my eyes. We locked eyes, and he whispered a prayer for me in the room before asking me to explain what happened. After the questions were complete, I was left in a cold room with just me and God, and I still heard nothing. I waited, I cried, and the silence became so loud that I started to scream. I asked God one question. "Why would you allow something like this to happen to me?" Nothing. I felt as though none of my senses were working properly and was eventually taken in an unmarked car to the side door of a hospital to complete a rape kit and an evaluation. Silly of me, I thought to myself, "Check my hearing because God sure is silent in all of this."

During the exam, many people met me in the room, like a counselor, a detective, and a nurse, and there were so many voices speaking at once, but I only wanted to hear one—the voice of my Father. I was taken to my parents' house in a police car, where my father locked eyes with me in the middle of the street as we approached their home and began to cry. I didn't speak, I didn't explain, but I went into my old bedroom, locked the door, and stayed there for days. I was waiting to hear something from God. I was desperate for a whisper. I remember drifting off to sleep hoping I wouldn't wake up from this nightmare. My phone had at least 40 missed calls from friends and family members after I didn't show up for events or class, but there was one text message from my best friend that gave me hope again. It said, "Fear not for I am with you, be not dismayed, for I am your God. I will strengthen you, I will help you, I will uphold you with my righteous right hand." - Isaiah 41:10. I read that scripture every day until I had the courage to confront the pain I was dealing with.

As the days progressed, I was still met with silence, but I also had the strength to sit in the silence and wait. I waited until I felt the presence of God fill the room. I waited until all my fears were chased away with the love of God, and I waited until I heard the whisper I was in desperate need of. "I am with you" were the words cemented on my heart that day and that ring loudly when I can't hear God, but I know He's nearby. At that time, no one knew the level of warfare I was enduring other than my parents when I would wake up screaming in terror and night sweats because I was still showing up for work, preaching in pain, smiling yet in sorrow but still living.

My best friend would send little reminders to my phone without knowing the detail of my despair as a reminder of God's love for me. Eight years passed, and I finally had the courage to tell my story of how my sister saved my life with her sensitivity to God. I was suffering in silence, but her prayers were a lifeline to my soul. I was able to live again and learned that in moments where we can't hear God audible, we can always feel him tangibly. We have a promise from God that he will never leave us or abandon us (Hebrews 13:5). My sister not only helped me heal throughout that time, but she helped me to hear again.

Bio

Crystal Arrington is a lover of God, counselor, author, prophet, and transformative leader.

As a coach, consultant, and counselor, Crystal has impacted and touched the lives of men and women through couch conversations and clarity sessions for the last five years. Known for her passion for deliverance, healing and freedom, Crystal's mission is to see men and women heal from past traumas, activated in their purpose and solidified in their identity. Crystal Rae Arrington is a native of Norfolk, Virginia, and a graduate of Old Dominion University, where she holds a bachelor's degree in psychology and human services, and a graduate of Regent University, where she holds a master's degree in crisis and trauma counseling. Crystal is currently completing her Doctoral degree in Clinical psychology and works as a mental health suicide and homicide crisis counselor. Crystal's greatest ambition is to empower men and women to gain stability in their hearts, minds, and in the truth of God's word.

In 2019, Crystal founded "Anchored Academy" mentorship program, where she assists men and women in their journey of stability in their hearts, minds, and relationship with God. As the founder of Anchored academy, Crystal conducts six-week online courses and training along with one-on-one mentorship for each student. In 2019, Crystal published and released her first book entitled "Anchored" and was afforded the opportunity to coauthor the anthology entitled "The God-fident woman," which became an Amazon #1 best seller in February 2022.

Chapter 2

My Sister Helped Me Heal
Nakia Triplett

I didn't know I needed to heal.
How does one become resilient when the stages of wound healing are unknown? I was raised to have it all together and depend on no man but depend on a man. As a woman, you wait on no one to make decisions that affect your day-to-day life; you move with your own and only best interest at hand, taking no prisoners all the while in bondage.

When I look at my life, I see a momma and a daddy but wonder how one can be fatherless. My dad would always say, "You know if you need me, I'm there," but in times of need, he didn't show. His inconsistency led me to believe this is the behavior of a man, which carried over into my adult relationships. And I better not complain; that wasn't something we did, show emotions that is. So, I went through life in countless unemotional relationships that resulted in unhealed wounds. Being so close in age to my mom, I didn't listen to the words that fell from her lips often in rage because of the unknown; I left at 17.

Life started then for me, street life. I now had to survive or listen, but being I'm one that doesn't follow directions, it was survive for me. I allowed the streets of HarveyWorld to mold me. I learned to live and think differently than the average girl. My name was not my name; my life was not my life. I found myself entangled in situations only God had the power to keep me safe.

A late night out disrupted my life. Months later, I found myself in the emergency room four months pregnant. Regardless of the ultrasound, I knew I was carrying a King. The baby shower was filled with blue boy Huggies diapers and about four pairs of baby Jordans. My bouncing baby boy was ready for the world, so I thought.

Then the labor started, healing process we'll call it. Twelve hours of labor I endured without any pain medication. I must say I took it like a G, not one tear until I delivered. It was at that moment my life changed, and I knew I had to redeem myself. I can remember my mother saying why are you crying now? It's over. I thought to myself, *No, it's not over; it's just beginning. I now have a responsibility. I now have a dependent. I now have a little person looking at me to feed, dress, protect and cover.* I decided not to raise my son King on the block. I now must obtain a career. There's a quote that says, "Change is inevitable; growth is an option." It was growth for me.

God's Purpose, Not Mine

While working overtime because child support was just not enough and due to me getting pregnant on purpose per King's father, he gave no additional funds. The money available was not what I was used to; college here I come. While working as a Phlebotomist, I met Corliss Taylor, who encouraged me to attend Nursing School. I worked full-time nights to ensure I attended all King's school activities and sports events. I was that momma that took him to and from school and, yes, home-cooked breakfast and dinner of his choice. He had real oatmeal in the morning, not instant, and was dressed to death. He was served just as he was named - King.

Just when I thought all was good, I met my now ex-husband. I spent ten years questioning my worth and trying to understand why this man kept leaving. I continued to pour into my son and career, resulting in a master's degree and pretty much saving lives as a Registered Nurse and in need of my own deep healing at the same time.

Live.Learn.Live

King and his father never saw eye to eye. I didn't push the issue because we weren't in a relationship, nor did he. At the end of the day, King is paying the price, but I'll take that one for the team. I should've been more responsible and better at choosing who I slept with. I tried to overcompensate with material things and allow the men I dated to be involved and shower King with gifts, but now that I look back, I made the situation worse. My prayer is that we do better with Baby King.

My Sisters

I have always been a churchgoer but not a Bible reader. One day working, I was invited by Bobbie Bension to attend Pastor John Hannah's church, and I was hooked. There was so much to offer to the broken, rejected, and abandoned; I knew I was healed. Well, until I started dating again, I joined the Victorious Disciples program and met my dear sister Zee Zee Cook, who taught me how to be specific and add scripture to my prayer. When alcohol was poured on those open wounds, I now knew how to go to the Bible, grab a dose and map out a treatment plan based on the stage of the wound. My sister Sherri Tillman shared the chalkboard that allowed me to have my favorite scriptures visible and names of individuals in need of prayer. Myriam McCoy increased my spiritual library.

My blessings didn't stop there; Zee Zee led me to Angela Martin, the prayer warrior that gave me the steps of prayer to capitalize on my healing. These wonderful women of God encouraged prayer, which pushed me to search for more like me, you know, with a swag. Someone I can call My Ryder, she goes by the name Destiny Inspire who encouraged me to speak and tell my story, all glory to God. Chavon, my Sis Speak Up partner, thank you for believing in me.

One special sister healed me like no other and endured a process that changed her life while giving life. On April 29, 1974, at 10:34 pm, this sister delivered a 3-pound, 14-ounce baby girl in distress. I call this sister momma (Sheletha MooreHarvey); thank you.

Resilience By Faith

I knew I was healed when I understood God is always first, then all else follows. I began to operate in God's will versus mine and no longer had to ask the question, why? My journaling became different; I started to command deliverance and loose positivity. I prayed for my enemies and loved those who didn't love me as I loved them. I stopped chasing to be healed and allowed the process to take place. In order to be who I was birthed to be, change had to happen, but not until I had completed the stages of healing. We must understand there are levels to this thing called life, and we're constantly evolving. This must happen every day for me until I close my eyes for the last time.

Who defines what I've become to be right or wrong and if I'm healed? No one.

Thank you, sisters, for helping me heal and not even knowing I was broken.

Bio:

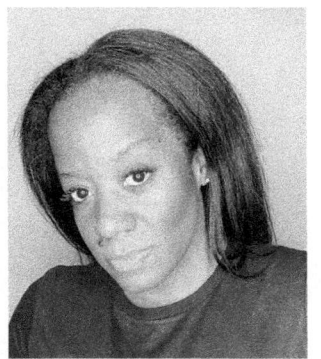

Nakia is a mother and grandmother, registered nurse, educator and thought leader. She loves to spend time with God by the water watching the sun set and rise. Faith and Integrity are philosophies that Nakia strives for in all aspects of her life. Nakia has served over 15 years as a Registered Nurse with a career experience in multiple healthcare settings. As the founder and CEO of Resilience By Faith, LLC Nakia has proven record of directly impacting the lives of people by assisting them recover from life difficulties by way of Faith and life experiences.

Chapter 3

Sisterhood: A True Definition of a Divine Connection
Cecelyn Dennis

According to the Merriam-Webster dictionary, the definition of sisterhood is as follows:

1. the state of being a sister
2. a sisterly relationship
3. the solidarity of women based on shared conditions, experiences, or concerns

For some, the above definitions for sisterhood seem like an ideal experience. However, in my life and the lives of many women, the experience of sisterhood has been everything but ideal! Growing up, I was surrounded by mostly boys. I have no biological sisters and a one older brother. Through my young eyes, it seemed that boys got more shine in my environment, so I wanted to be like one too! I wanted to be tough and adventurous, to be seen, heard, and valued.

I always had this soft, bubbly inner girl inside, but I rarely showed her because she was not as celebrated. The glowing, bubbly girl was often met with "who does she think she is?!" There were a few strong sisterly bonds in my family line. However, many examples of "sisterhood" I observed in my family and community were competitive and unhealthy. Then comes grade school through high school. I never fit in with the popular girls, mean girls, rich girls, quirky girls... girls, period. I spent the majority of my life feeling like the odd woman out.

Due to my early experiences, I believed that women could not be trusted and were drama-filled. I did not feel connected to most women and sometimes did not feel connected to the most important woman in my life... ME. As a result, I stuffed this part of me down, never to be seen again. Well, God had other plans! In college, thankfully, I met two amazing women I consider my sisters today. However, after college life happened and we went our separate ways, we still keep in touch occasionally. At 23 years old, I officially gave my life to Christ and was baptized; my roaring 20s happened... whew! Next thing you know, I am turning 30!

Interestingly, although I do not have a lot of close friends, I have a big network. I am a self-proclaimed popular loner! I began associating with women who were fun throughout the years, yet some of the influences began to hinder my walk with Christ and purpose. I felt like a Mary without an Elizabeth. One day, I felt the Holy Spirit tugging at my heart. I needed to surround myself with people who loved Him, loved me, and were in alignment with His plans for my life.

During this season, I also wanted a husband! One day, I made an unwise jest to God... "I don't need any friends; just send me my husband!" To my surprise, God dropped in my spirit that there were some old wounds in my soul as it relates to my femininity. He wanted to heal and unleash my inner femininity to add balance to my life, my whole being. A healed femininity would help me fulfill one of my purposes: empowering women. Also, it would add the gentle balance for me to be the wife that the husband I was praying for needs.

Sisterhood: A True Definition of a Divine Connection

In the fall of 2020, I decided to join the Pray For Your Future Spouse Challenge on Facebook. Keep in mind my sole intention was to get in there and pray for MY FUTURE HUSBAND! God is humorous because He had other plans. In other words, HE SAID WHAT HE SAID about healing my femininity!

During the challenge, we would write posts and encourage group members in the comments. One day, I saw a post by a woman named Brandi Weeks. She shared her testimony about her vow to remain a virgin until her wedding night as a woman in her mid-30s. She was vulnerable about being hesitant due to shame from perceived judgment about her age. I felt led to reach out and encourage her. I shared with her that her testimony is HERS, and it is powerful. I told her that there was nothing shameful about her vow to God regarding her age and virginity, and although it may not be the testimony for some, it will encourage many. Next thing you know, me and Monique Alexandrea Weeks, aka Brandi Weeks, became like two peas in a pod!

Our connection is truly divine. God sent. We have a lot in common. Yet, we are also delightfully different. We pray together, laugh, cry, encourage, shop, have fun… all those sisterly things! I found the Elizabeth to my Mary! In the Bible, Elizabeth and Mary had a special friendship and sisterly bond. They both encouraged and trusted each other with their most precious gift; their purposes within their wombs (John the Baptist and Jesus). "Blessed [worthy to be praised] are you among women, and blessed is the fruit of your womb (Luke 1:42 NLT)." To have a sister who genuinely acknowledges the favor of God on your life and is happy for you! The sister who speaks life over you! This is priceless.

Elizabeth had the humility to celebrate Mary, who had the great commission of giving birth to Jesus Christ! Brandi has this same breadth of genuine humility. There are days when I am Mary and she is Elizabeth. There are days when she is Mary and I am Elizabeth. Brandi has the Golden Retriever temperament [4 Animal Personalities], and I have the

Lion temperament. She teaches me to be softer and gentle in certain situations. I empower her to be stronger and ROAR in certain situations.

We offer a divine sisterly balance to each other. The new balance I have in my life is also healing my other relationships. Remember when God said He had some healing work to do within me? Well, He sent Brandi to help bring out the bubbly, gentle Cecelyn that He knows exists alongside the Lioness. Our sisterhood is a true definition of a divine connection!

Bio:

Cecelyn Dennis is a vibrant leader affectionately dubbed the Confidence Engineer. She is an Executive Operations professional in Wealth and Asset Management by trade. She is the creator of Creatively Cecelyn Enterprises by passion and purpose! She is committed to cultivating leadership that inspires others to creatively and effectively achieve their career and personal goals; Empowered, Self-Expressed, and Confident! Cecelyn has a Master of Science in Human Services Administration, a Women's Entrepreneurship Certificate, and a Certificate in Post Crisis Leadership.

Cecelyn currently resides in Atlanta, GA, although she is a proud JAmerican Princess who hails from the sunny state of Florida! As a woman of faith, she values the freedom in a relationship over religion (2 Cor. 3:17). The people closest to her describe her as vivacious, assertive, and fun-loving! She is a loving daughter, amazing sister, the "FUN AUNTIE," and proud fur-mama of a Chihuahua named Chica Belle.

Chapter 4

It's nothing Like Sisterhood
Monique Weeks

It's nothing like having true, pure, genuine friendships that turn into a sisterhood. True friendships are a blessing from God, especially if you do not have a sister. Sometimes finding a true friendship is rare and hard. It's difficult to build toward that space where you can fully trust someone with your deepest dark secrets, be yourself, and not have to change who you are. When you find it, or it finds you, you have to cherish it and, most of all, honor it. This type of sisterhood/friendship means the person will be there through the end of time no matter what happens. Ride or Die!!! That person will be by your side through the ups and downs, tell what you need to hear and not what you want to hear. Also, that person will always keep it real with you and never sugarcoat or lie. They will tell you when you are wrong in a loving manner and when you are right.

The saying goes, a person is not going to tell you the truth or correct you if they do not love you. That's what I love the most about genuine friendships that turn into a sisterhood. I value friendship a lot. I have so many friendships that I cherish. Sisterhood is sharing a special bond that no one can break and shared experiences. My name is Monique

Chapter 4

Alexandrea Weeks, and here is my back story of how I met my beautiful friend and sister, CeCe. I was in a very dark place in my life. I was dealing with deep depression, and at the time, I had just come out about almost taking my life two years prior. People around me that looked up to me were really shocked and upset that I did not come to them. I was so ashamed because I feared being judged because I am always there to encourage others and always there when others need me. I was so ashamed of thinking that my life was not worth it because I am a Christian, and Christian people are not supposed to think that way or do anything like this. That was one of the lowest points in my life.

I was stressed, dealing with the loss of my beloved daddy and working three jobs while helping take care of my mom and three nephews. I was also going to school for my Master's degree in Healthcare Administration. I never really understood true sisterhood the way I do now until I met my dear beautiful friend and sister, Miss Cecelyn Dennis A.K.A. CeCe. I met CeCe on August 28, 2020, while doing this Single's Prayer Challenge by Jamal and Natasha Miller called Prayer for your Spouse.

In the challenge, you had to post something about yourself and why you wanted to do this challenge. I posted this: There is nothing wrong with being Abstinent and waiting for your future spouse. It was a shame to let anybody know because the world and others had me thinking it was a bad thing to wait. I thank God for changing my thinking because it is a BEAUTIFUL thing to wait on the person God has for you because you're showing your love for God and your future Spouse.

December 30th will be two years since I renewed my Purity Vows to God, Myself, and My Future Hubby!!! Never let the thoughts of others make you feel that it is less important because it is important to God!!! I am proud to be waiting on My Future King, Best friend, and Hubby!!! I was super excited for five days of prayers for your Spouse Challenge. I was not going to post at first, but I changed my mind and posted my testimony about how I am saving myself for my future king and husband

and how at first, I was ashamed to be in my mid 30s and still a virgin and waiting.

Marriage is the goal, and I want my future husband to know that I love him that much to wait for only him. So CeCe direct messaged me about my post and how proud I should be because of waiting on my future husband. Most women our age cannot say this, and it is a blessing. I wrote her back and thanked her for the encouragement, and that's how our friendship/sisterhood started blossoming. August 28 will be two years that we have been friends. We pray together and for each other. We also pray for others around us. By meeting CeCe, I have grown a lot, and she has also helped me change my outlook on life and situations that arise. CeCe changed my viewpoint on some things like instant healing properly for your helpmate and learning how to let go and start investing in yourself. I can truly say that CeCe does show that pure, genuine friendship and sisterhood. She is a beautiful person inside and outside who has overcome a lot since we met. I am so proud of the woman she is becoming.

I am truly grateful to God for placing her in my life when he did. Cece has helped me overcome some of my fears and has pushed me to become a better friend and sister to my other friends. In this season, I am growing and learning that you must start putting yourself first and heal properly. We, as women of God, must be healed to allow God to use us. Since meeting CeCe, I have met more women and formed beautiful friendships that are turning into sisterhood. I want to leave the reader with this: healing is the very important key to becoming whole. Learn how to love yourself first, and the rest will follow; also, Keep GOD FIRST.

Chapter 4

Bio:

My name is Monique Alexandrea Weeks. I am the daughter of Mary F. Weeks and The Late Clifford Weeks. She is the granddaughter of The Oner and Idella Sherman- Gordon, Mae Weeks, and Joseph Rich. I have one sister Tara, two brothers, Chris and John, and many nieces and nephews, too many to count. I am a God-Fearing woman of God who has endured so many curveballs that should have made me quit, give up, and most of all, take me out. These life experiences have taught me that I am Worthy, Wonderful, and Beautifully made in God's image. He still loves me and will always be there for me. I will be totally honest with you. It has not always been easy, but it has helped me find my true God-given purpose: to pour into other beautiful women from all walks of life.

Chapter 5

You Waited Long Enough
Letitia Council

On the night of August 15, 2019, I was hit with a tragedy that I was forced to face. My oldest daughter was in a motor vehicle accident with life-threatening injuries. She sustained a hematoma to the frontal right side of her head, which caused Traumatic Brain Injury. The tragedy caused me to be face to face with pain, hurt, and frustration. Pain from trauma will have you feeling like you will never see victory. It will have you questioning whether you will ever allow God to help you heal. As parents, we don't think about preparing a homecoming for our children. God heard our cries, but before he heard our cries, He already knew the plans He had for Ja'Nasia. Jeremiah 29:11 (KJV) says, "For I know the thoughts that I think toward you, saith the Lord, thoughts of peace, and not of evil, to give you an expected end."

When I was faced with the tragedy, I couldn't understand for the life of me WHY this had to happen to my family and me? I wasn't living the best Godly life at the time of the accident. My daughter wasn't making the best decision as a young adult, but I couldn't believe we became face-to-face with a tragedy. Each day while my daughter was in the hospital fighting for her life, we had to sit still and be patient. Every day and night, the reports from the doctors sounded like they were the same, but God was the narrator of the report. Day after day, I had to process the challenge. I remained strong for my family. On the inside, I was torn to pieces. My husband could see in my eyes that what we were facing had shattered my heart, and it wasn't much he could do to repair the broken pieces. The hurt and pain I was feeling on the inside were masked up on the outside. I felt that if I remained strong and silenced the true hurt and pain on the inside, our daughter would feel that I was fighting right alongside her. We all have heard, "God allows things to happen in our lives for a reason." The truth is that at that time, I didn't know whether to believe that statement or not! Now that I have had two years to process what took place on August 15, 2019, fully, I believe God allowed the accident to give my daughter a second chance at life, although different from the one she lived before the accident. He also saved my life! Now I know many won't understand the statement, but truth be told, God saved a mother and daughter at the same time through a tragedy.

Later, in January 2020, God gave me The Nasia Foundation. That was the answer to my question in August 2019. A month later, The Nasia Foundation was conceived. That's when it hit me what my purpose truly was. On April 27, 2020, The Nasia Foundation was birthed. Not having any knowledge of running a nonprofit, I trusted God because I knew He would help me walk in my Godly purpose. And He did just that!

Just when I thought I was getting over the pain because I had said Yes to God! On the morning of April 25, 2021, I did Nasia's daily routine care and administered her medication. I was standing at her dresser with my back turned, and God showed me a vision of my husband and me standing at a casket. I then turned around, looked at Nasia, shook my head, and said, "No, not my baby. God not about to call her home." I then proceeded to do what I was doing. The vision came again. I shook my head again and said, "NO!" I walked over to Nasia, kissed her, and said, "Mommy is about to get dressed for church." Before I left the house, I said, "Okay, Nasia, mommy and your sister are about to go to church.

Your dad and brother are here with you." She gave me a slight head nod. I said, "I'll see you when I get back home." The time was now 9:45 am.

When I arrived at church, it was a little after 10:00 am. I walked into the church to assist in my assignment for that Sunday. My phone rang, and my husband told me I needed to get back home. Our lives were altered yet again. God called Ja'Nasia home to rest in His arms at the age of twenty. Nasia had gained her Heavenly wings and her reward. Now that was pain and hurt on another level. Ja'Nasia was my first born. There I was, full of pain that only God could ease.

Once I identified what I truly needed to overcome, I began to pray more, and God revealed to me that "I have already linked you to the sisters that will help you on this journey to heal." Those that were Godly assigned to me to help me overcome Fear, Rejection, and Lack of Confidence in myself, and removed the last two layers of the mask. I know I reached my healing because God spoke to me and said, "You have waited long enough. Your healing is a part of your self-value. You will no longer have to question if you are healed from the things that hindered you. My sisters uplifted me when God gave them a vision of me when I was down. They upheld me in the spirit and the natural. God has given me some amazing spiritual sisters, and I bless Him for that!

I began counseling two weeks later. That was a difficult decision, but I knew I needed to seek counseling to walk from pain into God's purpose FULLY this time. Walking from Pain to Purpose in God has allowed me to realize that all that masking up the pain can't go with me into my NOW, nor could I take the pain into my NEW.

Don't let your pain cause you to abort your purpose because of your emotions and feelings of fear and rejection. You don't have the authority to dismiss the plan God predestined over your life before you were in your mother's womb. March forth, the world is waiting for YOU!

Bio:

Inspired by a genuine desire to help others, Letitia Council, Founder and President of The Nasia Foundation, is a woman on a mission. She is a Traumatic Brain Injury and Caregiver Advocate who loves to share her story about her WHY? She encourages these women and assists them in rising from the ashes of their trauma. She has been blessed to be a part of many different organizations that support those in need. Letitia is a Newly Published Author, Amazon two times Best Selling Author, Inspirational Speaker, Certified Nursing Assistant, Certified Life Coach, and has an Associate of Occupational Science Degree in Medical Assisting. ACHI Award Winning Nonprofit Leader 2021.

www.thenasiafoundation.org

Chapter 6

Seeing Beyond What You're Saying It's in the Eyes or the Eyes Have It
Tracy Manley

I am convinced that our eyes tell a story far more in-depth than words could ever be. The old proverb that the eyes are the windows to one's soul could not have been a truer statement concerning me on December 25, 2010. This should be one of the most joyous days of the year; it was Christmas. The day we celebrated the birth of our Savior, the day that should have been filled with joy, laughter, exchanging of gifts, and Christmas dinner. Well, it was just a day that I wanted to come in quick and leave quicker. Of course, celebrating the birth of Christ was meaningful to me. Even as an adult, I still made my way into the house of the Lord that morning to celebrate his birth. The sadness I felt after the service caught the attention of my new First Lady, Gwendolyn Marshall. Who knew that this one encounter would not only change the trajectory of my life, but it would ultimately be the setup that God would use to anchor the next ten years of my life. I can still remember coming into church that morning and hearing the choir sing, 'Jesus what a wonderful child,' and how high the service was, only to remember that

Chapter 6

once it ended, we all would go our separate ways. On most holidays, my mom would work or volunteer to work.

Holidays had changed for her due to the loss of her mother and husband, and working kept her busy and kept her mind occupied as she coped with the holidays. Here I am 12 years later, and I finally realized what she must have been going through. I was so busy trying to find my way to happiness during the holidays while God was trying to send me daily help. I unfortunately never had the opportunity to meet my father, so the holidays were always one-sided.

Usually, I spent every holiday with my son's family, and this particular year everything changed, and I found myself missing what was. I did not know how to adjust to what was coming. As we all prepared to leave church that morning, Gwen came over to me and asked me if I was alright? It took everything in me to hold back my tears to tell her that I was fine. She did not settle with that answer because the eyes don't lie. William Shakespeare penned it best, "Our Eyes are Windows to the Soul." That Sunday, it was not my words that caught First Lady's attention; it was the emotions staring back at her through my eyes. Can I tell you that God has created women to be a bridge over unchartered waters, a shoulder to rebuild on, a listening ear that never judges, a hand to lift you before the world even knows you have fallen, and feet to direct you to a path that's already been promised to you! Because Gwen did not let my words overpower the sadness in my eyes, she continued with her line of questions. Looking back at it, all I can do is laugh because, over the years, nothing has changed. When Gwen asks a question, she will get an answer, and she's not letting it go, and that's just a small reason why I love her beyond words. She asked, "What are your plans for the remainder of Christmas Day?" I finally said I had none, and she asked if I would like to spend the day with her family.

I did not know then that my present pain was just the pressure needed to produce a 5-star friendship. That one invitation helped me close one chapter of my life and move on to the next. I foolishly thought our connection that day would be few and far between. However, I spent not only Christmas but Thanksgiving, birthdays, Easter, girls' nights in, Sunday dinners, and just about any day of the year at the Marshall's.

This particular year, the enemy used my biggest weakness against me: my heart. I loved family, friends who became family, and I was loyal to a fault. The enemy was so busy that he even had me believing that my own family was out of my reach. The truth was I was living an unhealed life. I was walking around with a broken spirit. I felt disconnected even in a crowd. I wore a smile on my face, but my eyes were empty. What I yearned for could not be fulfilled until I was refilled. I had hit a brick wall in life and needed a true friend. I needed not to be let down again; I needed an unconditional friend and literally needed a breath of fresh air.

I could go on for months about how Gwen came over daily to nurse me back to health after a major surgery, how she encouraged me during rough times in my marriage to stay the course, how she kept me grounded when our blended family was exhausting me, and how she would show up to support me without question in my many endeavors. She rebuked me or got me straight often; it was all in love. She would always say, "Now Tracy, or mostly now friend; you know you're wrong." Then she would say "You know when you are right, I got your back, but when you are wrong, I'm going to tell you." I honestly know I could not have made it through my first five years of marriage without Gwen and her daughter Kiera. Always a push but never a shove, always encouraged but never disgraced, always a helper but never a manipulator, always proud but never jealous, always my strength and has never left me depleted. I am proud to share that from the initial meeting, we have never disconnected and never had a day's trouble; now, for women, that's major. Even as our lives have moved us in different directions, this sisterhood is on lock.

Hebrews 24-25 NIV [24] And let us consider how we may spur one another on toward love and good deeds,[25] not giving up meeting together,

Chapter 6

as some are in the habit of doing, but encouraging one another—and all the more as you see the Day approaching.

Whatever life may bring, I know I can conquer it all with Gwen on my team. Scripture says that Esther was created for such a time as this but in my eyes Gwen was created in 2010 for such a time as this for me.

Bio:

Pastor Tracy Manley is the wife of Andre Manley, and together, they are the proud parents of one son Jaquan Smith and four daughters, Najae, Andrea, India, and Jada Manley. She is the daughter of Deacon Doris Hamlin and Marshall Pearson (Deceased). She pastors under the leadership of Apostle Yolanda C. Scott and Bishop Demetrics Scott of New Life International Fellowship of Churches. Pastor Tracy serves as the Campus Pastor of New Life of Moore Haven, Florida.

She and her husband proudly own and operate Manley Maid Inc., a Commercial Janitorial and Industrial cleaning company servicing Virginia and Florida. They also are the Co-Owners of Measure Me Non-Emergency Transportation Services.

She is the author of Access Granted the J3 Project as well as a Co-author of Women Who Rock Anthology.

Chapter 7

My Sister Fought for Me
Apostle Michelle Franklin

My life has literally been a roller coaster, especially when it comes to finding women I can call friends, let alone my sister. It seems like the moment I let down my guard, I was being betrayed. Not only betrayed but left uncovered. A real sister is one who covers you. She covers you in sickness, prosperity, and when character flaws are revealed. A real sister doesn't drop you in moments of uncertainty, disagreements, or adversity.

Growing up, I remember getting into an argument with one of my cousins who was drunk. She threw something at me. I got mad and threw the closest thing to me: my aunt's Bible. We started fighting. Two hours after we got finished fighting, she got into it with someone outside. No one had to tell me anything. I was headed outside to defend her. Why? Because we were family, and that's what families do. No matter how mad we are at each other, we cover each other.

We do that because we understand that as humans, we're not going to always get things right.

We live in a time when this generation's cut-off game is strong. All you have to do, is disagree with them, and not only are you excommunicated

Chapter 7

but your character is also assassinated. My prayer every year was, "God cover me. Teach me who to trust." I pleaded with Him to send me friends. Sisters in Christ who would have my back. As women, we need other women to teach us the way. That's why I believe in this assignment. There is power in sisters helping each other. For me, that starts with trusting someone to cover me. The question is, are there any women out there who understand how to cover you properly? Let's explore a few scriptures.

1 Peter 4:8 says, "Above all, love each other deeply, because love covers over a multitude of sins." Proverbs 10:12 "Hatred stirs up conflict, but love covers over all wrongs."

Imagine sitting in a movie theater during the summer months. It's one hundred degrees outside, so the theater has the air on high. So high you can't focus on the movie. Unexpectedly, your sister friend, out of nowhere, breaks out a blanket and hands it to you. Now you're able to keep warm and enjoy the movie. Covering keeps you safe and warm. It protects you from getting sick from exposure to the wrong things. By definition, covering means a thing used to cover something else, typically to protect or conceal it.

Today, the Lord has blessed me with a few sisters I now trust. However, there is one in particular that I want to give honor to. Her name is Alexis Ganier. We were always, in a sense, close. We trusted ourselves and had each other's back. On June 29th, I fell ill. I would reach out to her for prayer, and she always prayed. That Sunday, while attending church, I started going through deliverance. She was one of the first ones to run to my aid. Although there were so many around me crying out for my liberation, showing compassion, and comforting me, she stood out the most because I heard her voice. She instantly took my shoes off and started rubbing on my foot and legs, yelling, you're covered now!

Even if she never told me I was covered, I knew she covered me. She's the sincerest and strongest person I know. Her love for others is unfailing, and she gives it unconditionally. In this season, God has been sending me what I cried out for in the last season. He's showing me that

My Sister Fought for Me

I am worthy of true sisterhood. He's showing me that people can love you the way you should be loved. He's showing me that not everyone will give up on you and walk out on you.

One day, I was doing a study on compassion. The Latin definition for compassion literally means to jump in the ring and fight for you.

That's my sister Alexis Ganier. Visualize yourself fighting in a ring. You're losing the battle. All of a sudden, your enemies began to fall one by one. Just like when Nebuchadnezzar threw the three Hebrew boys Shadrach, Meshach, and Abed-Nego in the fire bound. While there, Nebuchadnezzar saw a fourth man who appeared to be the Son of God.

Alexis Ganier is that extra person you can count on to be in the fire with you. I believe it's an anointing that God placed on her. To stand and fight with people. For me, my sister helped me heal is about me being free enough to receive someone who was willing to help me. After being hurt by people, especially women, you get to a point where you no longer desire sisterhood. I told myself, "I got one blood sister, a sister-in-love, and a host of cousins. Who needs anything else?"

Apparently, I did. First, God sent me an angel to encourage me. Now He sent me someone who's fighting for and with me. In 2017, I lost my home in a fire, had open heart surgery, and lost three family members. Since then, I've suffered in silence because it's hard to be open, honest, and transparent with everyone as a leader. After all the rejection and losses, I had to fight to ensure I didn't take on an abandonment spirit. God needed me healed and to remain open for authenticity in others. Every day my mind would race with questions about why people would leave me. I saw women and men fighting to stay connected to abusive companions. Yet, the moment you say something wrong, step on their baby's toe, or refuse to support an unethical decision, they abandon you and assassinate your character. Although this is still happening in the world around us, I didn't let it destroy me.

I purposed in my heart to walk in forgiveness, so I won't lose my blessings. That's one thing to remember. The sisterhood you build is your blessing!

Bio:

Michelle Franklin has had the privilege of being trained by The John Maxwell Team, Dr. John Veal, and Dr. Anthony Tiller of American Christian Chaplaincy.

Michelle Franklin has demonstrated effective organizational and communication skills throughout her 19 years in Ministry and the Marketplace. She has exceptional leadership skills, management skills, and is considered a solution-oriented leader. She's skilled in critical thinking, conflict resolution, and a team player who encourages and influences leaders to mature and flow in one accord. She prides herself in building strong relational and interpersonal skills within teams and believes in professionalism and ministerial ethics to the highest degree.

Some of her experiences include counseling, coaching, speaking, teaching, and training leadership teams. She's a published author of 10 books and is set to release three more in the coming year!

Chapter 8

Coming Out of the Shadows
Karen Downing

Have you ever found yourself hanging back from the crowd, not really wanting to be seen, and definitely not wanting to be heard? Well, that was my story for most of my life until my Blessed, Obedient, Strong, and Saved (BOSS) sister brought me out of the shadows.

Let me go back to the beginning. I grew up in a loving single-parent household with my mom, Resia; my grandparents, Bennie and Janie and my older brother, Kevin, and I was always encouraged to do my best.

I can remember our grandfather often telling us "to be yourself" when we would leave the house to go out with our friends and even when I went away to college. I didn't have a true understanding or an appreciation of what he meant or why it was so important "to be yourself" until I got older and realized how peer pressure, wanting to please others, and just the world itself would have such a profound influence on my life and actions.

I would go on and do well in high school and even go to college and graduate. I never saw myself as one of the "popular" or "cool" kids. In most cases, I always tried to hide because I didn't want to be called out or singled out for anything. I was quite happy being in the shadows.

Chapter 8

My late mother taught me valuable lessons both by her words and by her example. One of her favorite catch-phrases was "birds of a feather flock together." Now, as a young adult, I had no idea what she meant, but I would listen when she spoke because I had learned early on to respect adults, especially my momma. It wasn't until I got older that I started to really appreciate her wise advice. I also learned that what she was trying to teach me even then was to be careful of the company I keep and be aware of those around me. 1 Corinthians 15:33 (NLT) says it like this: don't be fooled by those who say such things, for "bad company corrupts good character." Many of her teachings still ring in my ears today and keep me grounded.

I was a working adult before I learned about an extrovert and an introvert. My results of the Myer-Briggs Personality Test indicated that I was an extrovert, ESTJ, to be exact. An extrovert! Really! The traits of an extrovert are more of one having a preference for being around people. I was really baffled because I enjoyed living my life very much to myself and was quite satisfied (and comfortable) with being a "closet" introvert.

In 2006, God called me into ministry, and I preached my initial sermon on July 31st. To say I didn't know what I was doing is an understatement, but I trusted God and started on this faith walk to serve Him using what I would later learn are my spiritual gifts.

Spiritual gifts are funny, especially for someone new in ministry and who always wanted to stay in the shadows. Some of my gifts may have been in operation, and I wasn't even aware of them, and then others were nurtured and grew over time. There were things in church that came very naturally to me, and there were times when I saw how God would use me in certain situations to speak and exhort or to serve people that I didn't know or didn't know well. I went to church every Sunday, did what the Pastor asked of me, and served God through my preaching and administration, but something was still missing.

It wasn't until I connected with my BOSS sister, Frances, that I realized what it was. She helped me to see what was missing. Years of staying in the shadows, doubting myself, and taking in what "others" said about me had left me hollow and broken. Yes, I was serving, and yes, I was preaching, but I seemed to always retreat into the shadows right after so no one could really see me.

My BOSS sister began to talk with me, speaking life into my situations, asking me questions, and just encouraging me in my life (spiritually, emotionally, mentally, etc.). She could see things in me that I couldn't see in myself. She saw me as confident when really I wasn't. I would just do what I had to. Frances very much helped me to grow, similar to how Proverbs 27:17 (NLT) speaks of, "As iron sharpens iron, so a friend sharpens a friend."

In other words, she wouldn't let me stay in the shadows or the shallow places anymore. God is so much bigger than that! God is calling me to go out into the deep and to just trust Him even more. I can't stay in the shadows or where it's comfortable anymore. Luke 5:4 (NLT) reminds me, "When he had finished speaking, he said to Simon, 'Now go out where it is deeper, and let down your nets to catch some fish.'" God is still molding me, shaping me and smoothing out the rough places in my life. I know I am a work in progress, and it still boggles my mind that God would call me to Himself to be His daughter and a servant. I trust in Philippians 1:6 (NLT) that says, "And I am certain that God, who began the good work within you, will continue His work until it is finally finished on the day when Christ Jesus returns."

I believe that without Frances, I would still be "stuck" in the shadows without a voice, without work, and without joy. Sometimes it takes a change of space and people to be fully who God created us to be. It takes the love and acceptance of sisters who are not envious, fearful, or insecure to take your hand in the darkness and bring you out of the shadows.

I do not know where God is taking me in this season. I just want to be faithful and in a position to do what He calls me to do. I stand on Psalm 118:17 (NLT), "I will not die; instead, I will live to tell what the Lord has done."

Bio:

Karen is a native of the Eastern Shore of Virginia and has a passion for community that allows her to serve God and the people through the ministry of Jerusalem Baptist Church in Temperanceville, Virginia, under the leadership of the Reverend Richard A. Holland. Karen wears many hats in ministry and the community and does it all to the glory of God that lives may be changed and transformed. She desires to see others grow in the Word of God and serves as a Bible Study teacher and an instructor for the JBC Virtual Learning Academy. In addition, she serves on several local, regional, and state organizations, boards and committees. Karen is the daughter of the late Resia Downing and Louis Williams, a mother to Mykel, a godmother to Jakira and Steve, and a sister to Kevin and Monica. She stands on the scripture from Psalm 118:17 that says, "I shall live and not die to declare the works of the Lord," and prays that all she does would be to the glory of God.

Chapter 9

I Gave Him My Yes! Leaving Rejection Behind!

Leah Austin

When it came to giving God my yes, it did not come easy. I had to step back to reflect on what that truly meant. This would not be any type of yes; it was one that was the start of me getting off what I like to call the hamster wheel. If you were like me, you understand what that means: riding on something and not going anywhere. Although I was maturing and growing in Christ, God was blessing me along the way. I still felt like I was in this never-ending cycle of not going anywhere. I felt like I was walking in disobedience, and that is not a good place to be.

We all remember 2020, which was so long ago (LOL). Before the pandemic started, I talked with my husband about needing a change. I kept feeling like I was out of place. I felt like I was running in the same place and not going anywhere hence that hamster wheel metaphor. When we finally settled into it, I began to reflect on what I was feeling and why I felt that way. I have a great life in Christ, but I was still empty. As I began to pray and seek God, he would begin to reveal some past

Chapter 9

things in my life that I truly had not dealt with. He took me back to a time in my life when I was in college, and it was confirmed that I was pregnant. I realized I had to reach out and call my dad and mom to let them know what was going on with me. When I had to tell my dad that I was pregnant, that was one of the hardest things I ever had to do because we were so close. My dad and I were thick as thieves, and as a girl growing up, we would go everywhere together. I knew he would always have the answers for me, and it never failed that whenever I got in trouble or needed encouragement, everything was going to be OK because he would have the right words to say. However, it did not turn out that way.

There was such silence on the phone for the first time. He did not let me know it would be OK, and he did not have a word of encouragement. It changed our relationship, and we were not talking the same way as we used to. That was the same year my sisters in Christ led me to the Lord, and boy, that changed my life. However, as time went on, I did not realize that's where rejection started for me. It rode with me through life relationships and friendships like a bad rash a doctor could not remove. It made me question if I was doing things right. I felt like I could not make any mistakes. Of which no one can ever maintain this level of perfection. I remember when folks would say, "Leah, you are such a perfectionist," I would brush it off and think no way. But when I heard it a few more times, it made me think, *Is that how people see me?* because that is not who I wanted to be and not who I am. I am not perfect by any means, but I remember putting that perfectionist attitude on my family. All because I felt the pain of rejection in my life.

As I continued seeking the Lord in 2021, I remember feeling the spirit of rejection throughout my adult life which resulted in my hamster wheel journey. I met a young sister in the Lord named Chavon Annette. I did not realize that when I met her a few years ago, we would reconnect in the way we did. God led me to a "Fanning the Flame" conference for the first time she was hosting in Chesapeake. I knew it was God because

He revealed himself in such a powerful way through her as she spoke to me specifically about the things I was talking to God about, especially the rejection. Things I did not tell my husband. After that conference, I decided to give God my yes, and I was not going to turn back. It took me a few months to feel like I was not on that hamster wheel anymore.

Here it is 2022, and I began to set life goals because I gave God my yes and left rejection behind for good. He started to open doors that I could have never ever imagined. He began to set me on a path to hear him more and to follow his lead. Today, my relationship with my dad and mom is so amazing. I love it when my dad and I talk about the word of God and our faith in Christ. For a long time, I did not believe that could happen, but I can say God did it. Sometimes God must take you back to the place that we never dealt with for us to get off that metaphoric hamster wheel. Philippians 1:6, "Being confident of this very thing, that he who began a good work in you will complete it until the day of Jesus Christ."

As I continue my journey, God has connected me to meet new sisters in Christ in Power & Grace Leaders, Inc. This led me to start helping other women in my own church to grow in areas of their lives and walk in the freedom that God has given them. I know the ugly head of rejection when it tries to come back to my life, but by the power of the Holy Spirit and the relationships I have with my husband, family, sisters in Christ, and my church, this gives me the strength to carry my Yes forward.

Bio:

Special shout out to my youngest sister Robin Wiggins, who continues to encourage and inspire me to stay true to who I am.

Leah Austin is a servant of the Lord Jesus Christ. She's married to Wesley Austin with five amazing adult kids (Derik, Kenneth, Keith, Tiffany, and Aishlee) and her first grandbaby girl Lennox, whom she loves with all her heart. She's passionate about seeing women and men grow in the maturity of their faith in Jesus. As Discipleship Director of small groups and worship leader at Bridge Church, Virginia Beach, VA, she encourages others to walk out their gifts and talents. God has commanded each one of us to go and make disciples. She's a Financial Coach through the training of Ramsey Solutions, Inc. She and her husband also own and operate a catering business called "Weslea's Catering, LLC" (wes.lea.austin@gmail.com). Her mission is to see souls saved and believers grow in faith and be empowered by the Holy Spirit to do His good and perfect will for their lives.

Chapter 10

Birthing the Pain Through Victory
Marsha Johnson-Rollins

Jeremiah 1:5
"Before I formed you in the womb, I knew before you were born, I set you apart; I appointed you as a prophet to the other."
I remember this scripture said to me as a child, but I never understood what people said to me until I got older.

I want to speak to the woman wearing a mask to cover up her hurt, pain, betrayal, abuse, and feeling lost in this world. This was my story for 49 years. I walked around like I had it all together for years, being vital for everyone else and not being happy with myself. I was so lost in this world and, at the time, very suicidal. Let me tell you my story, then turn it into my testimony to my saving grace.

I was born in a little county town in Southern Maryland on December 14, 1970, and the hurt started when my mom left me at birth. Thank God for my grandparent who took on the roles and responsibilities of raising their first grandchild. As a child, I would wonder why I wasn't good enough for my mom and why she made so many broken promises to me. I would sit on the step waiting and waiting for her to come and get me, and she just never showed up. I wanted my mother to love me and couldn't understand why this lady didn't love me and why men and others came before. Don't get me wrong, my grandparent loved me, but that wasn't enough.

The most tragic thing happened to me three days before my sixteen birthday; I went to my cousin's house to get some belonging that she had of mine. As I was getting my stuff, my cousin's husband came in. I didn't pay it any mind. He was talking to me; before I knew it, he turned the light off and began to rape me. Once I could get away, I ran so fast to my house. I cried and cried.

I was able to call a family friend so they could take me to my grandma's job. When I was able to tell her what happened to me, at first, she guessed it had happened, and then she finally took me to the police station and the hospital. But the most devastating part is that she didn't want to press a charge against him because she was more worried about what people would say than me. I was so hurt and now even more lost in this world. I had to walk by the house each day and get cursed out by his wife, and finally, I moved because I didn't even feel safe anymore. So, I looked for love in all the wrong places for a decade of my life.

In 2001, I tried to kill myself and felt I wasn't good enough to be a mom to my sons; they would be better off with someone. I remember my pastor asking me while I was in the mental ward to write my obituary and the kind of food I wanted at my repast. I was startled by what he said, "Well, you wanted to die, so I was helping you." I knew I had to get myself together because I wanted my sons to feel loved, not how I felt. I went from one abusive relationship to another one because all I wanted to do was feel loved by someone. By 2004, I was a single mom with four children and three baby daddies.

I got married in 2010 to a verbally, mentally, and physically abusive man and had a mask on my face like I had the perfect marriage because I thought it was love. But I learned later that I damaged my children and brought anger into their lives by my decision.

In 2015, I was facing a legal battle that I didn't know would change my life so much. Some decisions I made when I was married came back, and now I had to face the judge. I was sentenced to seven months in jail. I cried and cried. I sat my children down and explained what was happening, and my sons stepped in to take care of their sisters. My youngest daughter had to be separated from them to go live with her dad. Being away from my children was so hard for me; being in jail made me even more lost. But that time alone made me spend more time with God. I had to deal with the emptiness in my life and the hole my heart had for forty-five years. I wanted to live. Happily, I tried to love myself finally. I wanted to be FREE of Bondage.

I remember writing, "I am a work in progress but still under construction." I started saying:

Because I am more than enough

Because I am beautiful

Because I am intelligence

Because I am great

Because I am more than a conqueror

Because I am King Daughter

Because I am a Boss

Because God said so, and it is so

I was released from Henrico Jail on May 29, 2017. I had lost everything: my home, car, and job. I had to start life all over, plus now I am a felony. At that time, I thought I had lost my career. When I got home, I was working for one of my church members cleaning a building, something I never thought I would do, but I did with excellence and treated as if it was that six-figure I no longer had. I had issues with my children and financial struggles. I cried many nights out to God for an answer. But finally, I put my complete trust in God. I took a job at Taco Bell than at the Noodles Company, but I worked these jobs daily with God's grace and mercy. I believed that God would open the door for me, and he did. I was able to go back to corporate America.

Chapter 10

It was NOT EASY

I believe sometimes we get caught up in the destination rather than what it takes to get healed and set free from whatever is holding us from reaching our true destiny. It's a choice we all have. As a sister, let's empower each other, let's love on each other, walk together, dream together, and most importantly, build together.

Bio:

Marsha Rollins, I'm fifty-one, with four beautiful children and four grandchildren. I'm a Senior Subcontract Manager for a Government IT Company. I love cooking, reading, and spending time with my family and friend. I am passionate about serving in the community and am currently on the Board of directors for a Community Outreach in Petersburg, VA. My goals are to open a reentry center to help rehabilitate women when they get out of jail. I want to be able to provide assistance with their healing, resume service, and assist in helping reunite with their children. I'm currently engaged to the love of my life and will be married on June 16, 2023.

Chapter 11

My Transparency, Their Love: The Tale of Many Caps

Melissa Daughtry

Wife, mom, daughter, church member, educator, entrepreneur, student, model, friend, and confidant. The hats, sis! The hats. There are many being worn, and I am sure I left one out. As I stack these hats or caps, I realize that I stack these bad boys as they come, not taking the time to see which one should be hung up for a bit. For a moment, I would like to put on my educator cap, then later, I'll switch to my "Girlfrand" cap (misspelling intended for extra razzle-dazzle).

There is a story I once read to my K-4 students called Caps for Sale. In this story, a peddler walks around with a stack of caps on his head, including his own cap, on his head yelling, "Caps! Caps for sale! Fifty cents a cap!!!" He would balance them perfectly around town while standing perfectly tall. One day, he sat and fell asleep, and to his surprise, all his hats were stolen by twelve monkeys. With frustration in an attempt to retrieve his hats from these mischievous monkeys, he ignored them, and they gave him back his hats. He walked off and returned to what he was

Chapter 11

doing, which was peddling the hats. As comical as it sounds, trying to get twelve hats from monkeys that are mocking you and laughing would be frustrating. But what happens when you have your caps, and they are the ones that seem to laugh and taunt you? Not a monkey, not a person, not even yourself, but the cap you carry… turns to you and becomes big, heavy, and even bully-like. I want to share how my "girlfrands" helped me carry my hats today with their love and support.

After reading my devotion and bible one Wednesday morning, I felt this overwhelming need to share my frustration in wearing my cap as a Believer. It's been about three years since I felt like all that I've believed in ended up feeling like it was more for others and not for myself. I looked back over the years of not setting boundaries, saying 'yes' to many things I didn't want to do and dimming my light so others could shine, and I got hot as fish grease. I asked God, "Why?" Why did he allow that person to mishandle me when they professed their love for me? Why did He not stop me from wasting tears and making repetitive mistakes when I tried to be a better steward of my money? Why did I not press harder to bring another baby into the world? Why??? Why God??? Oh, I got so frustrated and hurt until I moved farther away from God. I was close enough for Him to touch me, but also so far that I didn't want to touch Him. My heart was hurt. Hardened. Sad. Frustrated. The caps were heavy and grew heavier as time progressed.

The day before, I missed my therapy appointment. I thought I was going to begin the work of dealing with these feelings and begin the work of reconciliation. I needed to get closer to God. I felt it, and I yearned for it. The appointment wasn't needed because Holy Spirit told me to do one thing, "Talk to Monda and Zay." *Pulls out Girlfrand cap and goes to the group chat*

Voice quivering into a full sobbing vibrato, "Y'all, excuse my voice because I may burst into tears at any moment, but I'm hurt. I felt like God hurt my feelings, and I told Him," I said. "Not to mention, I'm terrified that if I get closer to Him, I'll get all soft and start to allow people to run over me! I don't want that to happen anymore! I want to be brazened, bold, set boundaries, and still be loving and soft. I just don't know how to do that!!!"

The next words sent by my "girlfrands" were words that melted me, "Thank you for your transparency and vulnerability! This is the realest thing I've heard... I am praying for you... I'm praying for all of us... I love you both soooooo much! Mel, thank you for choosing us to share and be vulnerable enough to say this because I've been feeling the same...." Sisters, I sobbed with my phone in my hand. They saw me. They understood me. They allowed me to be comfortable to come to them and share in my heartaches and frustrations. They and a small handful of others with the title of Sister wear the cap of family. Back in 2014, I lost the cap of Sister when my brother passed away from a heart attack. The love of a blood sibling is something truly special, and I thank God for allowing me a beautiful thirty years of wearing that hat. Can I say that God truly knows what we need and desire? Amen! So, He placed sisters in my midst. Not those I grew up with, shared clothes, and stayed late fussing about our parents. He sent other women; beautiful women who picked up a cap and offered me one, too. With some friendships spanning from 35 years to 3, God statistically placed these few women before me to love and share. I can't hide or act coy. They know me, see me, and allow me to be me. Proverbs 18:24 Good News Translation says, "Some friendships do not last, but some friends are more loyal than brothers." God bless those friends who stick closer than a brother.

So, those hats/caps that turned on me? My sisters showed me how to adjust and wear them proudly, just like her. And the ones she has that may shift a bit to the left or right, I help her with those. And here we are, transparent, loving each other, fixing each other's caps.

Bio:

Melissa Daughtry is the owner of Kabod Artistry, where she is a Professional Makeup Artist, Beauty Educator, and Beauty Influencer. On a mission to bring back the love of traditional beauty, she is focused on bringing beauty and beauty education to the "Mom-prenure."

In 2021, the opportunity presented itself to allow Melissa's work to be viewed by millions in the US. Her work has been worn by women entrepreneurs featured on shows such as Good Morning America, Women Evolve with Sarah Jakes Roberts, and some of our national Christian Networks.

Before becoming a Pro MUA, she was a former Pre-K Teacher and Governess of 23 years, holding an AAS and five Certifications in Early Childhood Development and has gained well over 700+ of training.

Melissa is affectionately the mother of AJ the Great and a wife of 15 years to Mr. Andre Daughtry, Sr.

Chapter 12

My Grandmother Helped Me Heal
Prophetess Deleigh Ryan

Writing this brings back a lot of emotions and thoughts that I have not revisited in a while. My Grandmother was a special woman. Unfortunately, she is now deceased.

Her name was Lucy Rosa Greene, affectionately known as "Mother Greene." She was a God-fearing woman, a preacher, an evangelist, a seer, and a prophet in her own right. She was a praying woman. I loved her. Here is the story of how she helped me heal. It was the summer of 2008. I was pregnant with my only son, Noah. At the time, I did not have any real support. I had no support from his father due to him not wanting to be a part of his life. I didn't have many friends, and the friends I did have weren't of much support except for one. His name was Drew. He was there at times when I needed him, but we were both young, and he tried his best just be that one person for me out of the group.

I didn't have the support of my parents because they disagreed with my pregnancy. I was alone, in my early 20's, in college, and trying to make sense of life. I am a fighter, not physically, but mentally and emotionally. All I knew was to push through, and this was the time in my life when I had to stand. I wasn't ready to be a mother. I knew I always wanted the typical nuclear family: husband, child, and a financially stable home. However, I had none of it. I felt like an unfit mother, an unprepared mother. God wanted me to have my son, in-spite of the lack of resources. To even support his desire, six months before I conceived, I had a vision of my child. Holding him smiling in a hospital gown alone. He was predestined. I just wasn't ready for the circumstances.

My Grandmother played a pivotal role in his coming. I had just recently rededicated my life back To God earlier that year. The rejection of loved ones, the gossip, and the laughter some of my friends did against me, caused me to turn to God. I knew how to talk to God, but I didn't know how to pray.

My grandmother, Mother Greene, was my Elijah and my lifeline. She showed me the way to God. It wasn't instructions with her teaching me. She didn't say "Leah, pray this scripture" or "Leah tell God this." I was just in her presence. She often prayed at 7 pm every day like clockwork. I would hear her speaking in tongues and crying out to God for her family. She had a white chair in her room for guests, and I would be still and listen. You see, I wasn't even my grandmother's favorite grandchild. We weren't close through the years. She had strange ways, but I knew she loved me. She would buy me gifts for Christmas, and comb my hair, I loved when she braided it. I would look at my hands and say, "Grandma, I have your hands." Our hands looked identical. I had moments with her, but I wasn't close. Not until 2008 did I see her purpose in my life. That year, and for the next two years after, I had many days with her. I could talk to her when I had no one. She would encourage me, listen to me, pray for me, and be still with me. Some days we would just watch TV together, 2020, the five O'clock news on channel 7, eat ice cream together, all the while I was pregnant with Noah. I didn't have a church. The church I attended rejected me because of my pregnancy.

My Grandmother became my Pastor, she became my friend. I never thought I would need her, but she saved my life. She showed me how to cook, bake cakes, and how to set the table within those last three years of her life. She didn't judge me; she just was there. One day I remember, I had just given birth to my son, and she came out of the room. I was going to my room next door. My son's father still hadn't come around, and I felt even lonelier than while I was pregnant. She looked at me and said, "I know I don't say much, Leah, but I understand, I understand." She knew the depths of my pain of having an absent father in my son's life because she went through it too with her children. That was really the day she helped me heal. Sometimes people just need the "I Understand." We are most effective when we speak of what we know through experience.

We had many more days together of sharing the word and prayer, more days after to eat ice cream and watch TV together, and more days to cook together. She was my friend. She believed in me as a mother and, one day, preacher. She was the first to tell me after washing my son's clothes by hand that I was a "good little mother." I loved her, and I still do. I am fortunate that God gave me her. I never knew I would need her the way I did in life. She was my friend and my grandmother, and she was my sister who helped me heal.

Bio:

Founder of Next Level Prophetic Ministries Prophetess Deleigh Ryan. A woman after God's own heart, Prophetess Deleigh Ryan, has served in many capacities in ministry. As a musician from the age of 13, as a Prophet, Teacher, Preacher of the Gospel and most recently an Elder, Prophetess Ryan has yielded to God. Her heart was always found amongst the music of God's house. However, the Lord had greater plans for her life. In 2012, she was released as a Prophet and minister and 2019 as an Elder in the Lord's Church. Also in 2012, Prophetess Ryan founded "Next Level Prophetic Ministries," which is her personal ministry. Under this umbrella, Prophetess Ryan also birthed "Soar in 2 The Prophetic Program," which is a prophetic school for all levels in the spirit. She also completed her studies at the infamous Fiorello H. Laguardia HS. She continued her education at Hofstra University, and Stony Brook University. A striver to be God's best amongst his elite, Prophetess Ryan's desire is to always remain humble and faithful to God first and his sheep. She believes without God and faith it is impossible to please him. Her strength comes only from God, and she firmly stands on Psalm 62:11, "Power belongs to God."

Epilogue

It was Necessary

Sometimes the things we encounter in this life are so devastating that we could not dare to see the necessity of the pain. Pain is always something that we try to avoid. There are not many people who volunteer to experience pain of any kind. However, in this life, we go through seasons of great pain, wondering how we will get to the other side. In the third volume of this book series, the women dare to share some of the most challenging and some horrific moments in their lives. When you look at them, you would not imagine they have some of the stories that they have, but it is all the grace of God. We are so glad that we can testify like the three Hebrew boys that we went through the fire that was meant to kill us but instead, a glorious testimony emerged.

These women took a risk to be vulnerable and honest, so the one who has picked up this book can understand that giving up does not have to be an option. These women are overcomers because of how they not only chose to survive, but they trusted God and are thriving. What would thriving look like for you? How do you define success in your own life?

Each day, we must make a choice to live. There are some seasons of life where the choice is easy, but other seasons of life are extremely difficult.

Epilogue

Who is in your corner? Have you isolated yourself because of the pain? Isolation does not benefit you; it is only an attempt to protect you from further pain. However, I have learned that pain is a part of life. I have also learned that through the pressure of pain, the best of me is produced with the help of God. Bishop TD Jakes taught that crushing produces the oil that God is trying to get out of you.

Whatever challenges you are facing today, know that God is with you to help you be victorious. In addition, God is stacking your life with divine sisters that will help you if you open your heart to receive.

When I began this series, I had no idea how much I would be blessed by sharing this journey with others. It has given me the beautiful opportunity to see just why God had me do this. I have learned more that people have been waiting for the opportunity to share their stories. They have been eager to encourage another sister who feels like giving up. It may sometimes be uncomfortable and scary as they have written their chapters, but they did what seemed like the unthinkable at one time. I'm proud of these ladies!

Revelations 12:11, "And they overcame him by the blood of the Lamb and by the word of their testimony, and they did not love their lives to the death."

Sister, put down your shame. Come out of the dark. Let your heart receive again. Believe better is coming. Release the need to be strong. Lean into God. BREATHE. Let go! If you made it this far, it's because God is not done!

Who will you take with you? Who needs your story? Who is waiting on you? Who said the next world changer couldn't be you?

Ephesians 3:20, "Now unto him who is able to do exceeding abundantly above all that we can ask or think."

I pray that after reading these stories, you walk away saying…
MY SISTER HELPED ME HEAL!

Visionary Biography:

First and foremost, Chavon Anette is a daughter of God! She is the CEO of Purpose Unwrapped, LLC and non-profit Power and Grace Leaders, Inc. Chavon is affectionately known as the Fire Leadership Coach and is a Leadership Consultant.

As the Fire Leadership Coach, she marries practical and spiritual tools to empower and equip kingdom people to lead in the world. As a Leadership Consultant, she partners with individuals, organizations, and ministries for leadership development and project management.

She balances entrepreneurship, ministry, and employment as the Student Success Manager at Regent University. She enjoys creating experiences for holistic transformation, so she annually hosts two big events: Fanning the Flame Experience and Powerhouse Leaders Conference.

She is also a transformational speaker and minister of the gospel who speaks with great passion in a way that empowers and challenges her listeners. She has been featured as a speaker on ABC news, TCT Today, Norfolk State University, Virginia Wesleyan University, and at conferences and other events such as globally recognized Comeback Champion Summit, Sister Leads Conference, and more.

Chavon has published four books that are available on Amazon, and she has been a part of seven anthologies. From Pain to Purpose was her first solo project that became an Amazon #1 Bestselling book. She is the visionary of volumes of My Sister Helped Me Heal Anthology, which is an Amazon #1 Bestselling Anthology movement.

Chavon Anette was the 2021 Servant Leader of the Year Award Recipient from ACHI Magazine.

www.ingramcontent.com/pod-product-compliance
Lightning Source LLC
Chambersburg PA
CBHW060034180426
43196CB00045B/2681